MW01596010

In
Montgomery

Books by Gwendolyn Brooks

POETRY

A Street in Bronzeville
Annie Allen
The Bean Eaters
Selected Poems
In The Mecca
Riot
Family Pictures
The World of Gwendolyn Brooks
Beckonings
Primer for Blacks
To Disembark
Mayor Washington and Chicago, the I Will City
Blacks
Gottschalk and the Grande Tarantelle
Winnie
The Near-Johannesburg Boy and other poems
Children Coming Home

FICTION

Maud Martha

NONFICTION

Report From Part One (autobiography)
Report From Part Two (autobiography)
A Broadside Treasury (editor)
Jump Bad: A New Chicago Anthology (editor)
The Black Position (editor)
A Capsule Course in Black Poetry (Co-author)

FOR CHILDREN

Bronzeville Boys and Girls
Aloneness
The Tiger Who Wore White Gloves
Young Poets Primer
Very Young Poets

In Montgomery
and other poems

Gwendolyn Brooks

THIRD WORLD PRESS
Chicago

Third World Press
Publishers since 1967
Chicago

ACKNOWLEDGING:

Poem 1 of "Winnie" was published in the 75th Anniversary issue of *Poetry*, October-November, 1987.

"In Montgomery" was first published in *Ebony,* August 1971, with Moneta Sleet's color photography, (See Note.)

First Edition.

07 06 05 04   5 4 3 2
Cover design by Borel Graphics

Library of Congress Cataloging-in-Publication Data

Brooks, Gwendolyn, 1917-2000
        In Montgomery, and other poems / Gwendolyn Brooks.
            p. cm.
        ISBN 0-88378-232-4 (alk. paper)
        1. African Americans—Poetry. I. Title.
        PS3503.R7244 I48 2003
        811'.54—dc21

                                2003050749

www.thirdworldpressinc.com

IN TRIBUTE TO:

my parents,
David Anderson Brooks and Keziah Corinne Wims Brooks,

my husband, Henry L. Blakely II,

my son, Henry L. Blakely III,

my daughter, Nora Brooks Blakely.

CONTENTS

NOTE

The poem "In Montgomery" was first published in John H. Johnson's *Ebony* Magazine – August, 1971. It was illustrated with the late Moneta Sleet Jr's splendid color photographs.

Moneta Sleet Jr. and I were sent to Montgomery, Alabama by *Ebony's* then Executive Editor Herbert Nipson. (The post is now held by Lerone Bennett; author of *Before The Mayflower* and other books, including the brilliant new *Forced Into Glory: Abraham Lincoln's White Dream*.)

Moneta Sleet Jr. and I would have a "planning breakfast," then we'd hit the Montgomery streets together. I would choose and chat with Montgomery citizens, pointing when sighting, and he would photograph them.

Of course, there were Civil Rights stars and starlets <u>chosen</u> for us to find, freeze and frazzle. Such as hero E.D. Nixon, Idessa Williams (voter-registration, there-at-the-beginning of the Montgomery Improvement Association, etc.) Ornee Patterson, Connie Harper, Irene Moore West, Nit Boll, Leon Hall, Dolores Boateng. <u>And</u> Mrs. Sallie Townsend – eighty nine:

> Oh I seen changes. My daddy told me
> "Everything is going to change."
> He say, "Sallie, you go' see
> changes I won't see."

Strangely lost to us – and much sorrowed over – was Moneta's heart-stopping feature of a solitary Black boy atop a tower of golden sand, in wonderful isolation – skinny arms spread in almost violent exultation, in exhilarated love of self and of the world.

Gwendolyn Brooks
June 20, 2000

In Montgomery

In Montgomery

The first thing I saw at Court Square corner
was Black, lifting that bale . . .

In Montgomery
when it was 1955,
when it was 1965,
when Martin King was alive and loud—
the civilrightsmen were many.
the civilrightsmen and civilrightswomen
hit it out as hatchets with velvet on.
Hatchets with velvet on.
With sometimes the hatchets hacking through.

White white white is the Capitol.
Inside the beautiful door
a Plaque in rich print which cites
sweet white supremacy's restoration.

My work: to cite in semi-song the
meaning of Confederacy's Cradle.
Well, it means to be rocking gently, rocking gently!
In Montgomery is no Race Problem.
There is the white decision, the white and pleasant
        vow
that the white foot shall not release the Black neck.

I came expecting
rags of old purple and gold,
old bloodboil,
King-images in every remembering eye,
and the King-song—"great hour!" "stride toward
        freedom!—"
still the stitching of every tongue.

I came expecting
the strong young—
up of head, severe,
not drowsy, not in-bitten, not
outwitted by the wiles of history.
For the old tellings taught me
that all of Before was rehearsal,
that the true trends, the splendors, the splurges
were to be lit by the young
(who would give up life, limb and the length of a
morrow for the Necessary Dream.)

I came expecting
the noble old
whose names would be WAY!
and DIRECTION! and STRIDE!

I did not come expecting in History City
the leaning and lostness,

glazed paralysis, and the
death-rattle of elderly vision
which met me in nice blue weather,
met me in soft sunshine
while cardinals glittered,
prettily threatening noses.

Montgomery is a game leg.
After such walking!
Montgomery is a smashed tongue.
After such Talking!
Montgomery is a peeled heart,
after such Feeling
The white folk are snug,
are snug.
Even after the "steppings aside,"
the Capitulations.
there is white snugness. White peace.
As in Peaceful Milk, Alabama, in Montgomery
there is white peace.

After the Grim Greatnesses.
an apathy rides the Blackness
in this little land.
To think of Montgomery is
to think of Blackness.

Blackness is what stood up
and clawed the oppressive ceiling
till, behold, there was light,
and clawed the oppressive walls
till, behold, there was room to extend!
Blackness remembered the Bible,
it was Blackness that re-said:
How forcible are right words!
and: Set thine house in order;
and: They have sown the wind, and they shall reap
the whirlwind;
and: A new commandment I give unto ye, That ye
love one another;
and: Weeping may endure for a night, but joy
cometh in the morning.
And Blackness stretched forth the rough hand
to the white hand.
and cherished it into the clearing.
This Blackness forgave what it would not forget.
And marched on remarkable feet.

Yet
into what country shall any go
and find **no** Likely thing?
Among those whose names are Flight,
and Lostness and Leaning and Empty-stare
and Final-howl-of-the-wind and Dragging-flag and

4

Whiner
and Struck-by-lightning and Dry-rot-in-the-heart,
there were to find
Justin
and Leon and Mildred, Dolores Boateng,
Idessa and Connie and Thomas Reed,
Jerry and Richard, Bouncing Betty and E.
D. Nixon . . .
Irene Moore West, and Lovetta,
and Sallie Townsend.
From twelve years old to eighty nine.

Mrs. Sallie Townsend
serves her Lord in Hickman Street.
She was born in Mamie, Alabama,
and in January was eighty nine, eighty nine.
Her father was Tyler Jones, her mother was Mary.

"You go to Bert's Drug Store
get Heart's Home Liniment.
'Cross street from Green! You go there.
Whatever ails.
Heart's Home will cure.
—And SERVE THE LORD! . . . Oh, I seen changes.
I had ten children. One is left alive.
That daughter there.
Oh, I seen changes. My daddy told me

'Everything is going to change.'
He say 'Sallie, you go' see
changes. I won't see it. You go' see
changes I won't see.'
And I see all them changes 'cep' one change
He say—there were to be a nation grow up high
        in the east.
that were to come through free in the world.
And I **know** that's one of the comings to be."
She is strongsweet,
a heavy honey.

Here's Justin, first Black page in Alabama.
Against majestic and special wood he stands,
loosely majestic and special.
A proper fit for the Situation!
The papers were made for his hands.
He is not overwhelmable (the
plaque on the wall in the entrance shakes a little.)

Leon Hall is twenty four.
His voice is eventful but it does not scramble.
Brown, clear eyes see you. They are not unkindly;
but there is not time for nonsense in those eyes.
Says Leon: "Overexposure it kills."
He is working in a consultant capacity
with the Southern Regional Council.
"I am pulling young people together around the
        south.

6

High-schoolers must know their rights. They must
        not fidget, nor scream
their time out." Says Leon:
"King outmaneuvered the white men. They have not
been outmaneuvered since 1955.
They infiltrate. They scheme,
spread rumors. Martin King
saw what was going on, broke it down
so all the masses could see and could understand.
Fifty per cent of our population's illiterate
and even the literate
are lulled by slick language, the language
whites use
to say they ain't goin' do nothin' at all."
Says Leon Hall:
"The same machinery that ran the bus boycott
is still here 'running' things and should
be carried out of things. It's a new day. Get a committee
together." He says to a
brown threshing woman who knows
Montgomery's muddy
and weeps, out of stretchy eyes,
as she thinks of Black children who labor in
mixed classrooms, for **love** from Black teachers
in the integrated schools.
"But love is denied them. I do not deny them.
I do not push them away. I do not turn,

7

with love in my look, to the yellow-haired.
Therefore, the little Black hand writes, wobblily.

'The best thing about school is my teacher.
The best thing about school is my **teacher.**'
Think of that!" Stretchy eyes
are really remarkable now for their wetness,
and up comes her linen to dry them.
"No!" snaps the brown threshing woman, resuming
firmness of fibre. "I cannot
stay in Montgomery.
No, no Committee.
I won't get a Committee together. I'm leaving
      Montgomery.
I must have Amusement. There is no one
to Amuse me. I must be amused."
Meanwhile, she weeps for the plight of Black children:
will speak, spurt and spar for Black children:
is spark plug, or spasm.

Idessa, Idessa Williams
is fifty eight years old.
She worked with voter registration, she
helped steer the original steering committee
of the Montgomery Improvement Association.
"Was there at Beginning."
Word-wayward and hard-eyed.

8

"A friend 'a mine tell me—
'Don't go in them folks' houses
talkin' with your eyes!"
Great days! Great days!
Black people came alive!
They put hands in
and pulled a Birthright out!
They dug into the storm
and scraped a sunshine from it!
Great days! But let
Idessa tell you:
the Miracle and Montgomery are dead.
"The light, it done gone out."

And what of white folks, Idessa?
"I use to hate 'em. Now I figure
they done done wrong so long
till they feel like their wrong way is the right way."
And what can rouse Montgomery, make revolt,
make passion, make a Bigness once again?
The Miracle and Montgomery are **dead,**
Idessa says she said!
The old guard's stiff. A resurrection?
The **young** folk **might** could yank 'em up alive . . . !

"Do you know that I represent."
says Thomas Reed, "the Governor,

the Lieutenant Governor,
and the Chairman of the Joint Chiefs of Staff?"
He is against smear-mail;
against electrocutions;
wants the president of this nation in Mississippi
(instead of murmuring that murder
of Jo-Etha Collier is madness,
the president should leave the White House tomorrow—
he should march in Mississippi;
his body should follow his words . . .)
What, in Montgomery, should Black men do
to electrify, polish, improve?
"We need victories. We need victories.
All parties must rally, come forward.
All Black men must make a togetherness,
decide on a Leader. There is
a break in communication. There is
a break in communication"
Thomas Reed smiles. His smile keeps a secret.
"There are first steps of the Black man,
registration; the determined knocking
on doors that are closed; and (mightily
meaningful) TRAINING."
Dark-dapper
against the White of the Capitol, he is firm.
"There will be changes," he vows.
(One of his changes is Justin.)

10

He was born in Bogue Chitto, Mississippi.
State president, NAACP.
"Many civic and business affiliations."
In November of 1970 he was one of the first Blacks
        elected
to the Alabama Legislature
        since 1874.
(Fred Gray is the other—Fred Gray,
once the protest movement's chief counsel.)
____Master of the minifilibuster!___
for his first speech, winning Ovation!
(though the enemy bill passed sixty-five to ten.)
"The **nigger** bill!—wanted white parents
able to transfer students
from assigned schools to schools of their choice
'if' the students are threatened or scared by their
classmates.
An affront to the Race, to the Race!"

Irene Moore West, with ear-holes for earrings.
White-silver hair is tight about her head.
Her
first certainty is that she's in the room
and Martin King's behind her in a frame.
She smooths her printed dress across her knees,
and looks at you a little.
She drove a car for a boycott.

11

the boycott days! "Many people for the first time
went to church!
I told 'em "Look nice!
Straighten your hair!
Take a bath!"
In Montgomery, are there many domestics?
"Not many. They don't want the old ones.
And they can't get, for the most part, the young
        Ones."
But back to the boycott days.
"Oh, there was prejudice.
There was meanness. I can assure you.
I went to Montgomery Fair. . . . they
didn't want my little granddaughter
to go to their **white**-ladies' room . . .
Kept up this talk-talk until
there was not **need** any more.
My granddaughter made her own bathroom
in the middle of the floor."
There is devil dust in old eyes.
But she folds her hands, is a Lady.
Old devil-flags are unfurled,
She says of her king. Martin Luther,
"He wanted to
humanize the world"

Mildred, Dolores, Lovetta

12

are twentyish, and
disturbers, devisers, deliverers.
But they pause! they demur, they gaze!
Revive Montgomery? Delineate?
Derail?
Invite a new vigor?
Dolores Boateng: "Ain't easy!
Montgomery's dead!
. . . . But maybe. . . . just maybe. . . .
Perhaps I could feed the poor.
Perhaps that could be my beginning."
Muses Loretta Walker:
"There are tragedies in this Movement."
Sometimes, it seems, a husband or wife
shows a differing eye for the movement."
Sometimes there is divorce. Or a killing;
or some other manifestation
of serious non-satisfaction—
"like, a lady sewed up her husband,
as he snored, in the snowy sheet,
then poured her boiling molasses
overall."
Mildred Smith shudders.
A scar on Mildred's forehead is faint now.
A white man tried to poke out Mildred's eye in the
Selma march—but missed.

Wit from the fortyish:
Benny, the basketballplayer of an older game-day
        says "Wallace
is smarter'n you think. He'll stand
in the door but he'll
get out of it, **too.**"
Benny winks. Montgomery's peaceful
Pretty peaceful. Except for the young.
They kick up a fit now and then.
On account of **them,** there's Little Incidents."
Why is that, if everything's peaceful?
"Well, what could be looked-over (**I** think)—
well, maybe they want to look into it. . . ."

Connie Harper directs
the Central Alabama
Opportunities industrialization Center,
one of the Top Five Manpower Programs In The
        Country
She "involves the total community"; provides
vocational and pre-vocational training.
Training for young and old, for male and female.
        And the motto is
"WE Help Ourselves."
Connie Harper is sturdy, secure
and proud; her practical warmth
is like a halo above her, it

floats in accompaniment, glows
when Connie glows, and knows
before she knows
what is required of Connie any morning.
At 3114 Caffey Drive,
across the street from an efficiency green "project."
the typewriters quick-click away, in the typewriting
        class.
A song of dry delight.
Each was bought "by involving the people."
by "enlisting the total community.
We help ourselves. We recruit,
stride into the street and tell them
the meaning of O.I.C.
The people enroll in the Program.
And before you know it they're learning.
and before you know it they're earning. . . ."
(And out strewing wisdom and wealth in the world!)

"What people need
is a self-survival kit." She recommends
"spirit to **want** to survive."
The O.I.C. . . . . . ."
_____So many hurdles and pitfalls!
She has to beware.
"I am wary.
For white men think me attractive. . . ."

She is attractive.
She has to admonish **with care**. . . .
Connie
is the mother of Justin, that first
Black page of Alabama.

E.D. Nixon. Of whom Martin King
in "Stride Toward Freedom" said:
". . . . never tired of keeping the problem before
the conscience of the community.

When others had feared to speak. . . . had spoken
with courage. . . . . had stood
with valor and determination. . . ."
Long Blackness leans
against the Rest he feels he quite deserves.
E.D. Nixon, name two young Montgomery Blacks
from whom
inspiration, **good** action may spring!
"I can't name **one**."
E.D. Nixon fits fingertips, neatly.
"We ought to be buildin'.
Burnin' ain't going to help.
Where are the young folks that's buildin'?
These young folks will come in to dance.
No dancin', no young folks.
Maybe they want to be "Teacher"—
but that's their highest ambition.

Two things your people haven't learned:
you can dignify any job—
and you can be totally illiterate
and still be intelligent."
He induced, it seems, Reverend King
to take his place as chider, cherisher, champion.
First to organize a campaign in Montgomery
to get Black men to register, vote.
Elected "ten or twelve" times
to be Alabama president of
the NAACP. Solicited
successfully the aid of Eleanor Roosevelt
(who was a passenger on "his" train)
"toward equal recreation in the armed forces,"
and launched
the first attempt to integrate the schools
of Montgomery, Alabama.
He organized, at the Holt Street Baptist Church,
        in the basement,
on December fifth, in 1955,
the first meeting of the
Montgomery Improvement Association.
"Headlines said 'four thousand five hundred
hymn-singing Negroes.'
My estimate: seven thousand."
He mentions the mind of "a darned good lawyer
not liked by too many people. . . ."

We are driven, now, in an air-conditioned car
through the hot and bright blue weather.
There is
new construction on Highway 65.
On the West Side of Montgomery
at the top of a mountain of sand a Black youth
is astride the Future!—looks up and out and away.
At the bottom, Mark Franks, Joseph Duncan,
          James Robertson
feel "ain't too much wrong with the South."
but are leaving—"cuttin' out"—for New York,
or North ("not South") Carolina.
"Or there's army. Get into the army, good ol'
career can be made out of army. . . ." "You see?"
says E.D. "You see?"
. . . . But then.
at "his" Boys' Club on Boys' Club Road,
there's Ornee Patterson, friendly,
a student at State, and laboring
"in business administration" . . . .
In the car, E.D. Nixon
fits fingertips neatly, remembers:
"King said, when I called, 'Let me think
about it, and let me
call you back'. . . . and I said to myself
I'm going to hang him to a star."
_____**What** was your first Motivation?

"The Auction Block in St. Louis
made the skin crawl on my bones."
There is Memory in his eyes.
"Some call me 'Uncle Tom,' says E.D. Nixon.
"I'm not Uncle Tom. HOWEVER,
there were **great** Uncle Toms in the old days.
They were helping their people—and **knew** it.
You take these new Uncle Toms!
Get one a job in a bank!
Turn white overnight. Want nothin'
to do with you anymore. . . ."
In Madison Square Garden
E.D. Nixon had told 'em
**"Fifty thousand Negroes began to ROCK that Cradle
and segregation started to fall!"**
E.D. Nixonisms:
"Montgomery was a pilot light for the nation.
(A **pilot** light never gets larger . . .)
Sure, we want to be 'militant,'
sure, we want to 'progress.'
But we've got to have jobs, because people
who do not work will steal."
And E.D. Nixon says that
"To make a might of a movement
"you need a Resolution, and a Name. . . ."

Wanted:
        The Fine Hand of God:
        Marching Songs for the People, in a
Town that Could Be (But Ain't) Your Own.

There are so many Black people!
The streets are a-swarm with Black people.
It is hard to believe what the Census says
(in a
Town that Could Be, But. . . .)
Downtown, Saturday afternoon. . . .
Afros, cloud-downy (with a comb in this bush of a
        male!)
Bright stripes in insouciant trousers.
Red blouses. Red dresses.
And pink, purple, loud white, and green.
Mutter-murmurs and shouts;
and insults to thin maidens, who love them!
Wide women a-waddle.
A preacher, erect, but self-conscious among
these the Children of God gone, most likely, astray
(with "pot," perhaps in a pocket, and
worse wickedness in mind.)
        Tender babies
        Each numbered!
        Each leashed
        with many establishment leashes.

20

Smiling
in the bloodily pretty world where
kinships go crazy.

A sleek long brown dog
is dead in the middle of the street.

So beautiful. Through moving.

Bench-sitters, waiting for buses.
What do you think of Montgomery?"

I am asking under
large eyes of the Whitley Hotel.
First National Bank, the Jefferson
Davis Hotel, in History City.
(The catcalls of history hang in the air:
niggers! black cows! black apes! black scum!)

"HELP KEEP MONTGOMERY CLEAN" This sign passes
by on a Blackman's back.
"There is a need for someone to show the way."
A full figure. There is power in the face but the
stitches are loose.
"We needs someone to organize us."
A fire-cracker beside her, in clothing angrily clean:
"There's always goin' to be bloodshed

if we's to get anywhere.
Especially since
we done sent up prayers
and been real good
and done gone through all that sufferin'.
God is a righteous God.
He look down peaceful on all.
But JESUS get **MAD!**
JESUS'll get up and DO somep'm."
Power-in-the-face: "Old glory gone by.
If we would just start it again,
and keep up the sparklin', keep up the sizzle.
then we would be
in the gloryness once again."
Fire-cracker: "They still
want not to wait on you in they stores.
They wait on **me,** however. If I want somethin'.
I just say Hey, you! And they come.
They BETTER wait on me."
_____Another view. Spent man, with frozen yellow
        in the eyes.
Old pepper's in the middle of cold yellow.
Black, bent he is, long has been, ever shall be.
"Ain't nothin' wrong with Montgomery
You can go **any**where you **want** to. You can go
in **any café.**
Any café.

You can go
to the ball game
You can go
to **any show**"
The pert small wife says "Amen."
_____Nit Boll:
"There's room for improvement."

Black female strides are defiant, or sassy,
or tremulous. Some of the young
are indifferent to anything white,
are focusing on tonight's date
or tonight's collard greens and corn pone.
"Scrupulously" clean,
they wait for the bus in front of
the Milner Exchange Hotel. . . . .

Nit Boll:
"There's room for improvement.
The little money you make don't do nothin'.
The little money you make
don't go nowhere at all."
Any changes? "Well.
You can sit down now.

You
can sit down beside 'em at last."

(Leon remembered sitting-**in**,
The hate, the heckling, the pain,
"They threw us out to the street, but
we went to the counters **again**.")

A spear of a Black girl
in a glass-green skirt, tight, tiny
below her sleeveless white blouse.
She is Real Cool, munches candy,
flicks a comb
through the short black wires of her hair.
She examines tan sandals on feet
that were made to frolic through jungles.

The Paper Bag Brigade.
There is a prevalence of paper bags.
clutched, wrinkled.
We've bean-eaters here! Grease is often their
hollandaise and their consoling.

Jerry Johnson in his dark glasses,
Richard Muse in his stripes.
Leon Hill in blue jeans—
are rail-sitters at the First National.
"What do you think of Montgomery?
Do you plan to stay here, and build?"
Young Richard Muse will be

"goin' up nawth where the money is." Young
Jerry Johnson's not sure. Leon Hill
looks off and away. . . . . . .

Near Sears.
In a Nice Neighborhood.
Bouncing Betty is raking. White mistress
mows, and is quietly pleasant. . . .

At Sears,
white Misters Kitchens and Payne are kind
make it easy to see our Black
sisters and brothers at work in this shiny store.
Warm little
Je Cynthia Bethea in **stationery-beads-and-boxes.**
William Sankey in **furniture.** Brenda Moton
in **housewares,** Jay Houser
in **paints.** Observes Mr. Payne:
"Other are here and there. . . ."

I ride on a bus.
There is only one line on Sunday.
The "Black" line.
"Ninety nine per cent Black bus riders."
says the Black bus driver; "and you
can have a 'bout-empty bus
and some of them Black

still sit in the back.
Built into 'em. Can't get rid of it."

At the Dexter Avenue Baptist church
in History City, Martin King
gave the True Bread to his People.
Now Murray Branch,
heartening, handsome,
is the provider, and the True Bread.
"which comes down from heaven, and gives life
to the world" (New Testament), is strengthening still.
It is served quietly
to "The Beautiful People" of Montgomery.
Here is a hat made of red flowers.
Here are the soundest wigs.
Blue abounds, and print, lace, and ribbon, and
costly straw abound.
Here
are boys-of-whom-their-families-are-proud.
Mild usherettes in ivory and white.
They read aloud the "'59 Covenant
to refresh our thinking about the
mission and glory of this Church."
"Wash-stain" windows. Pale blue walls (a peaceful
hue) white ceiling, in joined squares. Hanging glass
oblongs of a simple, elder dignity.
Long center carpet of a warm red weave.

The pew aisles, scrubbed clean wood.
Nothing is amiss.
Hymn 312—"I Am Thine, O Lord (Draw Me Nearer)."
I Am Thine, O Lord, I have heard Thy voice.
And it
told Thy love to me. But I long to rise in the arms
of faith, And be closer drawn to Thee. . . .
Adds Murray Branch: "We are feeling beings before
we are thinking beings. We are sensate beings be-
fore we are logicians (if we EVER become logicians)
The slaves found correspondence between the Scrip-
tures, especially the Old Testament, and the religions
they had known in Africa. The Christian
religion is a SINGING religion."

Murray Branch tells, and has told, his people
"Don't sit down on the job.
Dying while still ambulatory
is reprehensible!"
But Montgomery is mostly still
still.

WABX, the Soul station,
"Come ON, sing the SONG this Mawnin'!"
The Soul Stirrers sing the song.
_____WABX is bemoaning
Astronaut-talk of a Government Visitor

to Alabama State University
". . . . . . which had NUTHIN', but NUTHIN' to do
with Black folks. . . . ."
**"O Happy Day! (when Jesus washed, oh when
He washed. . . . my sins away!)"**

"The Old Ship of Zion!"
WABX is pleading:
"Try to feed somebody who's HUNGRY
Try to clothe somebody who's NAKED.
Try to visit somebody who's SICK or in PRISON.
Won't cha?"
The Soul Stirrers sing. . . .

Martin Luther King is not free.
Nor is Montgomery

A FARMER

A farmer —
at the times he doesn't have anything to do with animals__
Is very close to the meaningful sweetness of things.
Altering the earth with glory.
Making furry wheatstuff come out of the earth.
All furry in furrow, miles across the scene.
Putting corn **Up**, cabbages **Up**.
In fine masterful Putting.

Now it is October.
Here is the black black earth.
Prepared by the selfsame farmer.
Combed.
Oh lovingly lovingly.

He steps this way, and that.
Reverently.
His seamed cheeks tighten and rest, by turns.
He is intent, but not hurried.
The sun beats upon him. His cancer began long ago.

<u>Something needs tending!</u>
Readily,
his body a prayer,
he kneels.

Monday October 24, 1988.
On Amtrak train to Osceola.

29

BEHIND THE SCENES

When I see a President, a Vice President, a Secretary of
State on sparkling tile,
beside noble columns of white,
I think to myself: "Somebody got there early,
and swept, and scrubbed; somebody dusted."

Before the President came,
somebody buffed his shoes.
The not too-stiffened white of his shirt
was not achieved by his own agility.

At the invisible controls: some little
weak-kneed, stricken, or powerful woman or man.

A Girl

There was A Girl
who set forth upon waters of life,
of living.

There were black stars set in the
blue-whites of her eyes,
before which all populace Gasped and said
"The whites of your eyes are blue."
She was gracious and grateful.
Meagerly, she nodded.

"There are enemies in the waters of Life"
it was said by those people, that populace.
"When they get you they will gut you!
Sometimes, when she heard this (one among
certain languages) Girl
would take overmuch time to shudder;
but later was fit; and again
would go on.

July 21, 1998

AN OLD BLACK WOMAN, HOMELESS, AND INDISTINCT

1.

Your every day is a pilgrimage.
A blue hubbub.
Your days are collected bacchanals of fear and self-troubling.

And your nights! Your nights.
When you put you down in alley or cardboard or viaduct,
your lovers are rats, finding your secret places.

2.

When you rise in another morning,
you hit the street, your incessant enemy.

See? Here you are, in the so-busy world.
You walk. You walk.
You pass The People.
No. The People pass you.

Here's a Rich Girl marching briskly to her charms.
She is suede and scarf and belting and perfume.
She sees you not, she sees you very well.
At five in the afternoon Miss Rich Girl will go Home

to brooms and vacuum cleaner and carpeting,
two cats, two marble-top tables, two telephones,
shiny green peppers, flowers in impudent vases,
visitors.
Before all that there's luncheon to be known.
Lasagna, lobster salad, sandwiches.
All day there's coffee to be loved.
There are luxuries
of minor dissatisfaction, luxuries of Plan.

                3.

That's <u>her</u> story,
<u>You're</u> going to vanish, not necessarily nicely, fairly soon,
Although essentially dignity itself a death
is not necessarily tidy, modest or discreet.
When they find you
your legs may not be tidy nor aligned.
Your mouth may be all crooked or destroyed.

Black old woman, homeless, indistinct__
Your last and least adventure is Review.
        Folks used to celebrate your birthday!
Folks used to say "She's such a pretty little thing!"
Folks used to say "She draws such handsome horses, cows
and houses,"
Folks used to say "That child is going far."

September, 1992.

Gottschalk And The Grande Tarantelle

GOTTSCHALK AND THE GRANDE TARANTELLE

My Black brothers and sisters.
Nimble slaves in New Orleans,
dancing to your own music,
loving your wild art,
your art, vertical, winnowy, willful—
you did not know that Gottschalk was watching, was
        hearing.
Slouched in the offing, he was.
Crouching most shamefully, he was.
Stealthy. Heavily breathing.
He fell in love with your music.

Died at forty.
But before that he Created
Le Banjo (An American Sketch.)
He Created
piano pieces based on slave dances.
He created
piano pieces based on "tunes he heard in the Congo."

Early he stole
the wealth of your art.
Wrongfully
he bore it away to the white side of town—
you never knowing—

and there he doctored the dear purity.
He whitened your art,
and named it his own.
He traded it for money
in Great Halls of whiteness.

He sold it to thronging white company.

The patrons went MAD.
Loving odd music (embroidered savagery),
women wept and wilted.
They cut off and wore his hair.
He became the Lapel-piece Composer.
His concerts and conquests multiplied, he handled
        many a money,
and he died at forty, an over-musicked man.

He rose *across* you, Black Beauties.
He stole your art.
He never passed you a penny.
Nor painted your name on a page.

But *hark!*
He inherited slaves from his father and freed them.

All hail the Debt-payer.

WINNIE

Winnie Mandela, she
the non-fiction statement, the flight into resolving
        fiction,
vivid over the landscape, a sumptuous sun
for our warming, ointment at the gap of our wounding,
        sometimes
would like to be a little girl again.

Skipping down a country road, singing.

Or a young woman, flirting,
no cares beyond curl-braids and paint
and effecting no change, no swerve, no jangle.

But Winnie Mandela, she,
the She of our vision, the Code,
the articulate rehearsal, the founding mother, shall
direct our choir of makers and wide music.

Think of plants and beautiful weeds in the Wilderness.
They can't do a thing about it (they are told)
when trash is dumped at their roots.
Have no doubt they're indignant and daunted.
It is not what they wanted.

Winnie Mandela, she
is there to be vivid: there
to assemble, to conduct the old magic,
the frightened beauty, the trapped wild loveliness, the
crippled reach,
interrupted order, the stalled clarity.

Listen, my sisters, Brothers, all ye
that dance on the brink of Blackness,
never falling in:
your vision your Code your Winnie is woman grown.

I Nelson the Mandela tell you so.

II
SONG OF WINNIE

Hey Shabaka.
Donald and Dorothy and William and Mary,
Angela, Juan, Zimunya, Kimosha.
Soleiman, Onyango and Aku and Omar,
Rebecca.
Black Americans, you
wear all the names of the world!

Not a one of you ex-Afrika Blacks out there
has his or her Real Name.

I know.
You are alive. I know.
You wake, and you like the sun.
Water on your body is healing and is dear.
On your cereal the butter-rivulets
make morning art.
You prepare your hair, you
stride into the outer morning, you
are crisp and resolute and maximum.
You
don't disorder the décor
by looking at it too hard.

Well,
you don't know my people.
You don't know Keorapetse,
what he bears, has borne.

We organize our funerals.
The government has not decided
whether or not to let these latter funerals take place.
The government may decide to go ahead
        and let those funerals proceed.
The government has not yet
made up its Mind . . .

I, Winnie, want
those funerals processed and resolved.

There is so much in my head.
Lilliesleaf; the Special Branch; and Zindzi . . . .

Childhood had a skippingtime but mostly
cow-milking, goat, and sheep, and hefty prayer,
my little sister's sickness and her death, my
mother's fierce mothering of her Given Nine,
my mother's furious faith, my mother's death,
my father's leading, modest, subtle-sassy,
my father, wise-warnful: "Get you back The Land!"
Childhood had a skippingtime but mostly

I learned to bond the faith-steam of my mother
and the retrieval-passion of my father
and the thriving bloodfire of the Pondoland people.

I try not to love me.
I try to be at big remove from me; I try
to do the good thing always because it is good.
I try not to worship my prettiest piece of pottery.
I try not to judge my berry-blue headband
a better band than Brigalia's.
The people in the roads who bow-to
are warmed by what waits in my eye for them.
There is no art, no guile, no craft, no cold breeze in
        my eye
to be a chopper or a going-down for them.
They say of me
"She has to fix people."
They say of me
"Hers
is a large hard beauty."

Our monsters are smashing the children.
No ribbons or shells in the childish hair?
God must have a really fierce appetite for puzzles.

I want some settlings of these puzzles,
I want replies to whys of the human condition.

Why cannot I just go ahead and live?

43

Why must I keep High Arrogance at the ready?
I reverence our children.
It is bracing to be in the company of our young.
They Had the nerve to believe in common sense and
goodness.

The beasts with terrible faces
are impervious to humanitarian concerns.
Humanitarianism is for other countries.

To be mechanic, automatic, Quick—
this is the way of the Time of Evil.

We have, of course and also, our Black "Statesmen."
They pour forth.
For indeed they are full.

Every day we are losing dear persons.
One of the griefs of losing,
through death, a dear person,
is that you have no longer the old delicious reasons
to say out the good Name:
"Mama!" "Sisi Vuyelwa!"
or "George!"

I used to listen to the Elders.
"Winnie! be a nice girl!
Be a Nice Young Lady!" . . . .

The difficulties of being a Nice Young Lady—
and reformer/revolutionary/pioneer!
"Strongwoman" too.
It is true I am partial to stripes.
I admire my striped scarf (and that headband.)
My Xhosa robes are sensual.
I know that I am a beautiful woman.
But Ladyhood . . . .
Ladyhood eludes me:
nor shall favor me ever.

When Botha's lieutenants
spit in my face, and pinch me,
Ladyhood eludes me.

The beasts with sick faces whom
we allowed in our land, in our living places—who
proceeded to poison our rooms—sometimes decree
there will be no singing.
(You can be shot for singing.)

Flowers, thistles, grasses,
leaves—and winds
to blow them sweetly . . . .
Oh there is so much calling and murmuring and
        pulsing and beating about in my head.

In dreams
I *think* I'm always firmly what I know myself to be.

White pelicans in Uganda,
dipping beautifully
and in unison to
achieve their fish . . . .
There is, still, loveliness in the world:
in Uganda: in Kenya:
even here—
this home
heart-halting, perverse.

There are millions of words in this world.
Not necessarily may be found, all cooked,
the ones to express *my* nuances.

Yet I know
that I am Poet!
I pass you my Poem.

A poem doesn't do everything for you.
You are supposed to go *on* with your thinking.
You are supposed to enrich
the other person's poem with your extensions,
your uniquely personal understandings,
thus making the poem serve you.

I pass you my Poem! — to tell you
we are all vulnerable—
the midget, the Mighty,
the richest, the poor.
Men, women, children, and trees.
I am vulnerable.
Hector Petersen was vulnerable.

My Poem is life, and not finished.
It shall never be finished.
My Poem is life, and can grow.

Wherever life can grow, it will.
It will sprout out,
and do the best it can.
I give you what I have.
You don't get all your questions answered in this
        world.
How many answers shall be found
in the developing world of my Poem?
I don't know. Nevertheless I put my Poem,
which is my life, into your hands, where it will
do the best it can.

I am not a tight-faced Poet.

I am tired of little tight-faced poets sitting down to
shape perfect unimportant pieces.
Poems that cough lightly — catch back a sneeze.
This is the time for Big Poems,
roaring up out of sleaze,
poems from ice, from vomit, and from tainted blood.
This is the time for stiff or viscous poems.
Big, and Big.

I tell you from Ice, from Vomit, from illegal Blood:
It is Ridiculous For These Many Millions of Blacks,
In Their Land, In Their Land.
To Waltz To the Tune Of The Limited White Music,
And This Cannot Go On.

I am wild. I am strange. I am stiff and loose together.
There is slant there is vault there is strut there is jangle
        here in my head.

Even so essential spirit
lapses not, nor lags.
I continue my mealie in morning.
I continue to cherish my Various people.
I Lean Into, I Prop, I Proclaim my people.

In the Land of the Black People
the sun comes up.

As the sun comes up in other lands
so up comes the sun in the
Land of the Black People.

When they write about me,
it is of a giantess with her hands on her hips.
When they sing about me, the
notes are sweetish, are fond, are redemptive, are
         talisman.

But they are the notes to salute
the Upright Tree, praising it for withstanding blows,
not for moving
an inch out of hell;
(look around: the fires are rising, are flirting
         obscenely, they are
doing a crazy backward and forward and back again
         dance.)

I *would* be *not* the "Upright Tree."
I *would* be the little skittering Ant,
intelligent and important and questing—
impeccable . . . .

              IMPOSSIBLE!

That is impossible.

I (sighing) accept my fate.

I am here to assemble, I am here to conduct
interrupted order.
I am Code (not Ant). I am (says my Nelson)
woman grown.

I am meat and dessert for my people!

Each one of my people has the right to enjoy, the
        right to require
the Health and peace and gentleness of the body.
The language and levels, the nominations of the soul.

I countenance never
the killing of Other Animals in the sacrificial
        splendors.
The Metaphor is not to be missed, not evaded.
There is a dizzy whizzing in my head.
There is a writhing in my head.
Hector Petersen is residential there.
Hector Petersen: thirteen and dead,
shot in the back at Soweto,
on June sixteenth, in 1976.

Nelson is residential there.

Do I love Nelson?

I came to Oracle long ago.
Puzzling on "what is Love," I came:
Oracle, I wish to know
if what I feel for Certain So-and-so
is Eternal Love. If not, I'll leave the thing,
the search continuing.
Oracle revealed an eye of flame.
Must things have names? Shall there be tags for gold?
Be glad if, when the glances touch, they hold.
If it is cleansing blessedness to meet
be glad-and call it "sweet."
And if perhaps-quite naked of a name-
your Feeling finds you reaching for *his* hurt
to cool, crying for that, pity alert,
if you would die for him, or think you would,
be proud, and call it "good."

I never came to Oracle again.

Nelson is residential in my head.

We were human together.
We were frolicsome and merry, we rubbed noses;
        we giggled.

We were clear bells together.
"You have a little trotty walk," he said.
"You are also grand, also a queen," he said.
"You are a quip and a quirk and a queen," he said.

I was frisky but became what he named me, After:
high-souled Family shepherdess.

(I do not like to coronate myself.)

He taught me how to love and to let go.
He taught me how to taste a darling song
and rise from little table satisfied;
how to enfold good people
and not take fright, anticipating Loss.
Tutored by him, I do not grab
addresses, telephone numbers.
Tutored by him, I touch the temporal
with fingers used to losing.

Serpent Emerging.
Enter Serpent.
No garden is immune.

Do you remember Nelson straight and free?
He had an editor's eye
for the malformed, for the indistinct.

He circled our clichés.
Before his people he was eloquent.
He was not fearful. Confronting his people, he knew
an audience is a bunch of ones;
that he was not entreating
a gang, a mob, a smear of faces,
but was driving
to and into each set of secret graces.

Civil and strangely international.

Our durable Assembler.
Our voluptuous Wrangler.
Co-falterers, we stretched
in the tension of his composure. Then we
danced to the light of his signal flares.
The harmed heart meritful.

Nelson. Nelson . . . . .
Our youth is spent!
Taken from us.
His hair graying, whitening in prison.
Almost three decades gone.
He,
a grandfather.
He,
a luminous antique.

Sometimes he envies "ordinary" people
who have no debt to words.

Sometimes himself he censures, disavows
his name and marrow: "I have 'let' the monsters
master me! I, Nelson, Champion of my people!
I am this Champion, underpressed in prison!
Useless to my people!"

A luminous antique.

"Sometimes I tell Me
the Struggle is a Wiggle."

(But *right* is the luster of that heavy age.
Issuing from seclusion, special fire
to inspirit the weary and the far-away.)

And I?
I am a woman waiting.
Mine is a stately waiting, also a walkie-talkie waiting
transmitting and receiving.
My waiting does not whimper, does not whine.

I, devoted to and admiring of my husband,
stand tough-on-my-feet. I

am Today's Woman. Today's Woman
is not ward nor toy nor curio nor game,

nor slavey in this sun-time of the monsters.
Sisters! We are meritful,
and are—before an end—perceptive.
We are hurt honey but we do retrieve.
We do not squirm, we do not squeal. We square off.
We blue-print
not merely our survival but a flowering.
That's good. Because the Plight is serious in
this field of electrified spikes and boulders.

We join our men and memories of our men.

With clean effective faces we proceed,
civil when possible,
in right response to
the thousands of little/big
approximations, seals and breakings of seals
and whithers and eithers
that stuff our days.

In this country
every day
death calls us out to put a stop to him.

We are Tilted;
but have no need to imitate the imitations.

We shall
      think—
      plan—
see the day whole through our assaulted vision,
prepare for surprises, little deaths, demotions.
big deaths,
all sorts of excellent frictions and hard hostagings.

Ultimately Daunted Down we cannot be!—
anciently
coming from some order of organic
peace and mist and mystery.

We are Tilted;
but we are The Choosing People.
Ours *is* the Favorite Truth, we *are* Truth-tellers.

Truth-tellers are not always palatable.
There is a preference for candy bars.

Waking earlier, we
devise our next return
to sense and self and mending. And a daylight
out of the Tilt and Jangle of this hour.

THINKING OF ELIZABETH STEINBERG

   Friday, November 13, 1987.
Already you're on Page 8.
And in a while your name will not be remembered
by that large animal The Public General.

I don't know *who* will remember you, Lisa,
or consider the big fists breaking your little bones,
or consider the vague bureaucrats
stumbling, fumbling through Paper.

Your given name is my middle name, Elizabeth.
But that is not why I am sick when I think of you
   There—
no one to help you in
your private horror of monsters and Fools.

You are the world's Little Girl.
And what is a Little Girl for?
She is for putting a bow-ribbon on.
She is for paper dolls.
She is for playmates and birthday parties.
She is to love, to love.
She is to be precious, precious.
She is for ice cream cones.

She is not to be hurt.
She is not to be pounded.

Elizabeth, Lisa.
We cannot help you.

They wept at the wake in Redden's Funeral Home,
among messages, bright gladiolas.
There was weeping at your grave.

Tardy tears
will not return you to air.

But if you are Somewhere, and sentient,
be comforted, little spirit.
Because of your lean day,
the vulgarity of your storm,
the erosion and rot of your masters, sitting in the
          sputum of their souls—
another Lisa
will not die.

You help us begin to hear.
We begin to hear the scream out of the twisted mouth,
and
out of the eye, that strives to be Normal.

We shall listen, listen.
We shall stomp into the Horror Houses,
invade the caves of the monsters.

In the name of Elizabeth Steinberg.
In the name of
Lisa.

MICHAEL, YOUNG RUSSIA

To Mikhail Kusmenko, twenty-one years old.
From a Black Woman
born in America—whose origin is Afrika.

Michael, I see you!
In the Russian winter.
The lights in your quick, smart eyes
are dancing with snow-sparkle.
You ski; you skate over the ice.
In your heart you shout
"I *breathe*! I am *alive*!
My body is moving!
My body knows life is good and my body responds!
I am a straight response, a Reverence!
And I love all the people in the world!"

Michael—
I see you in the woods of Moscow and Kiev,
affectionate with deer and branch and flower.

Young Russia!
You are an affectionate spirit,
with arms stretched out to
life and love and truth and Celebration,
with arms stretched out to
what is clean and kind.
Thursday, July 29, 1982, Kiev.

BRELVE. A BATTERED WOMAN.

She began the Marriage
with exhilaration.

She chose, with live care,
saucepans, a blue roaster,
a set of silverplate from Marshall Field,
a lace tablecloth (headed for Heritage!)

He had smiled. He had felt her.
He was bright for the wedding.

Bright for the week, the two weeks. The four. She
could not believe The First Blow.
She could not believe
the arrival of her own loathing:
nausea behind her eyes:
the fear of a memorized footstep:
ice in vein and brain.

The descent of dream.
The dried-out drum-beat of desire.
The slams of doors down Corridors.
Decay of construction, of old construction,
scrupulous and confirmed.
End of love. End of love.

But presently, presently,
the self-wrought hour of self-confrontation
and small steps to a
raw resurrection.

New Shapes of hospitality to Self.
New architecture in another morning.

60

Brooke Maj, Of Hawthorn South School

Brooke:
you wore little silver shoes,
you walked in magic.

Today
you are real and not real.
We shut our eyes and we see you.
The premiums of our alliance
are to keep! — to adjust,
to consult and sort over,
to add to our life and, therefore,
to your own.

Note: "Maj" is pronounced MY.

THE BEAUTY IN THE FOREST

(December, 1968)

And even deep into the forest
the beauty was — where No One could see.

The Forest Beauties
perfected themselves
for no gaze.

BLACK LOVE

Black love, provide the adequate electric
for what is lapsed and lenient in us now.

Rouse us from blur, Call us.

Call adequately the postponed corner brother.
And call our man in the pin-stripe suiting and restore
him to his abler logic; to his people.

Call to the shattered sister and repair her
in her difficult hour, narrow her fever.

Call to the Elders—
our customary grace and further sun
loved in the Long-ago, loathed in the Lately;
a luxury of languish and of rust.

Appraise, assess our Workers in the Wild, lest they
descend to malformation and to undertow.
Black love, define and escort our young, be means and
        redemption, discipline.

Nourish our children—proud, strong
little men upright-easy:
quick
flexed
little stern-warm historywomen. . . .
I see them in Ghana, Kenya, in the city of Dar-es-
        Salaam, in Kalamazoo, Mound Bayou, in Chicago.

Lovely loving children
with long soft eyes.

Black love, prepare us all for interruptions;
assaults, unwanted pauses; furnish for leavings and
        for losses.

Just come out Blackly glowing!

On the ledges—in the lattices—against the failing
        light of
candles that stutter,
and in the chop and challenge of our apprehension—
be
the Alwayswonderful of this world.

LAST INAUGURATION OF MAYOR HAROLD WASHINGTON

The time there was no time to anticipate
        came anyhow.
        Sleep. Sleep.
        Every hour was worth the
tightening of purpose and vein.
You swept the city courtyard responsibly every day,
every day you Charted, you Chastened.
The circular ripples are riding, are Reaching —
        beyond interrupting.

        It is good
        You came.

11/29/87

DUKE ELLINGTON

The man is forever.

Blue savoir-faire.
We loved that. We loved
that dukehood. We loved royalty and riff
because we could not reach them for ourselves.

We loved. We love.

He built a fuzzy blanket all around us.
He fed us, in such Ways! He
could educate us toward fulfillment,
reduce our torrents, maim our hurricanes.

We listened to that music:
our caterpillars instantly
were butterflies. Our sorrows
sank, in sweet submission.

He provided philanthropy
of profound clouds, provided
shredded silver and red, provided
steel and feathers.

We have him!
The man is forever.
We have forever
his sass, his electric Commitment,
his royalty, his Love.

MARTIN LUTHER KING JR.
April 4, 1968

A man went forth with gifts.
He was a prose poem.
He was a tragic grace.
He was a warm music.
He tried to heal the vivid volcanoes.
His ashes are
          reading the world.
His Dream still wishes to anoint
the barricades of faith and of control.
His word still burns the center of the sun,
          above the thousands and the
          hundred thousands.
The word was Justice. It was spoken.
So it shall be spoken.
So it shall be done.

JANE ADDAMS

I am Jane Addams.
I am saying to the giantless time—
to the young and yammering, to the old and corrected,
well, chiefly to children coming home
with worried faces and questions about world-survival—
"Go ahead and live your life.
You might be surprised. The world might continue."

It was not easy for <u>me</u>, in the days of the giants.
And now they call <u>me</u> a giant.
Because my capitals were Labour, Reform, Welfare,
Tenement Regulation, Juvenile Court Law (the first),
Factory Inspection, Workmen's Compensation,
Woman Suffrage, Pacifism, Immigrant Justice.
And because
Black, brown, and white and red and yellow
heavied my hand and heart.

I shall tell you a thing about giants
that you do not wish to know:
Giants look in mirrors and see
almost nothing at all.
But they leave their houses nevertheless.
They lurch out of doors
to reach you, the other stretchers and strainers.

Erased under ermine or loud in tatters, oh,
moneyed or mashed, you
matter.

You matter, and giants
must bother.

I bothered.

Whatever I was tells you
the world might continue. Go on with your preparations,
moving among the quick and the dead;
nourishing here, there;
pressing a hand
among the ruins
and among the
seeds of restoration.

So speaks a giant. Jane.

DANNY GLOVER

Danny Glover is
a good poem.

This poem tells us what is new and old.
This poem reinforces, clarifies
and dares.

This poem is
an aspect of utility
bold, braced, and brave.

Danny Glover
is a today-poem.

Memorize him joyfully and well.

ASTONISHMENT OF HEART

> The Lord shall smite thee
> with madness and blindness
> and astonishment of heart.
> The Bible

There was a thick roaring in the forest.
High muttering through the trees.
        We shook at what others had told us
of monsters crouched in the mysteries.

Snorts. Rasps. Harsh halloos.
Flickering eyes.
The padding of impatient paws.
The monsters would maul us efficiently,
sink in us teeth mottled, and crusted with blood.
It was enough to chill more experienced children.

But we shook our heads. We withdrew. We would not believe.
After all, we were Handsome, and we had Withstood.
Our faces were clean, our nails were polished and long;
and we had been playing our games, and we were languorous,
and our eyes were dulled with cigarette smoke and our
mouths with song.

They stepped, the monsters, out of the darkness,
ate some of our kind.
The monsters, stepping out of the darkness,
ate some of our kind. They were quite what the Others had
said.

And they were
the others.
And they

resembled ourselves.

It was Truth. It was not a nightmare
with waking to wait for and coffee-and-Danish in bed.

OLD WOMAN RAP

Peg

Things are different now.
I'm not strong.
I don't <u>wanna</u> go out in the yard
To see what's wrong.

I don't <u>wanna</u> mow grass,
For the sun to scorch.
I don't <u>wanna</u> govern the gutter
Nor paint the porch.

I just wanna curl myself into
a little-old-woman ball.
Or smile to myself, or eat cherries or catfish
In a clean room away down a hall.

7/15/90

FOR SARA MILLER, SCULPTOR

      Sara, thank you
for Extending my life;
for sending my life into bronze
and beyond—
as a clean pride
not to be tamed, not corralled.

You see beyond seeables, see
beyond flesh,
beyond motion, images, beyond the hard burning.

No longer walking through rooms,
I shall be gone and not gone.

ART

Art can survive
the last bugle of the last bureaucrat, can survive
the inarticulate choirs of makeiteers,
the stolid in stately places,
all flabby gallantries, all that will fall.

Lending our strength to keep art breathing we
doubly extend, refine, we clarify;
leading ourselves, (the halt, the harried) through
the icy carols and bayonets of this hour,
the divisions, vanities, the bent flowers of this hour.

We hail
what heals and sponsors and restores.

PATRICK BOUIE OF CABRINI GREEN

What is devout is never to forget.
Never to shelve the value and the beauty.

Patrick.
Vivid. Valid. Lyrical.

We cannot reach,
We cannot touch.

The radiant richness that was Patrick
Cannot be reached again, cannot be hugged.
        Cannot be visited.

What is devout is never to forget
that he was with us for a little while.
Our splendor.
Our creative spirit.
Our sparkling contribution. Our
flash of Influence interrupted.

        Our Interrupted Man.

Children Coming Home

Speak the truth to the people.

Mari Evans

AFTER SCHOOL

Not all of the children
come home to cookies and cocoa.
Some come to crack cocaine.
Some come to be used in various manners.
One will be shot on his way home to warmth, wit, and
                              wisdom.

One teacher mutters "My <u>God</u>, they are gone."
One is ripe to report Ten People to the Principal.
One muses "How have I served or disturbed them today?"
One whispers "The little Black Bastards."
One sees all children as clothing: the blue blouse —
the green dress — the tight-fitting T-shirt.

One will take home for homework each of the
twenty, the thirty, the forty one.

TINSEL MARIE

JAMAL

RICHARDINE

NOVELLE

KOJO

ULYSSES

MERLE

SALA

GLADYS

AL

BUCHANAN

MARY FRANCES

FLEUR

DIEGO

MARTIN D

CALVERT

TAHANNI

ARON

SUPERBE

NORA

Tinsel Marie

THE COORA FLOWER

Today I learned the <u>coora</u> flower
grows high in the mountains of Itty-go-luba Bésa.
Province Meechee.
Pop. 39.

Now I am coming home.
This, at least, is Real, and what I know.

It was restful, learning nothing necessary.
School is tiny vacation. At least you can sleep.
At least you can think of love or feeling your boy friend
against you
(which is not free from grief.)

But now it's Real Business.
I am Coming Home.

My mother will be screaming in an almost dirty dress.
The crack is gone. So a Man will be in the house.

I must watch myself.
I must not dare to sleep.

Jamal

NINETEEN COWS IN A SLOW LINE WALKING

When I was five years old
I was on a train.
From a train window I saw
nineteen cows in a slow line walking.

Each cow was behind a friend.
Except for the first cow,
who was God.

I smiled until
one cow near the end
jumped in front of a friend.

That reminded me of my mother and of my father.
It spelled what is their Together.

I was sorry for the spelling lesson.

I turned my face from the glass.

Richardine

WHITE GIRLS ARE PECULIAR PEOPLE

White girls are peculiar people.
They cannot keep their hands out of their hair.
Also
they are always shaking it away from their eyes
when it is not in their eyes.
Sometimes when it is braided they forget —
and shake and shake
and smooth what is nothing
away from their shameless eyes.

I laugh.

My hair is short.
It is close to my head.
It is almost a crown of dots.
My head is clean and free.
I do not shake my head to make
my brains like a crazy dust.

Novelle

MY GRANDMOTHER IS WAITING FOR ME TO COME HOME

My Grandmother is waiting for me to come home.
We live with walnuts and apples
in a one-room kitchenette above The
Some Day Liquor Gardens.

My Grandmother sits in a red rocking chair
waiting for me
to open the door with my key.

She is Black and glossy like coal.

We eat walnuts and apples.
drink root beer in cups that are broken,
above The
Some Day Liquor Gardens.

I love my Grandmother.
She is wonderful to behold
with the glossy of her coal-colored skin.
She is warm wide and long.
She laughs and she Lingers.

Kojo

I Am A Black

According to my Teachers,
I am now an African-American.

They call me out of my name.

BLACK is an open umbrella.
I am Black and A Black forever.

I am one of The Blacks.

We are Here, we are There.
We occur in Brazil, in Nigeria, Ghana,
in Botswana, Tanzania, in Kenya,
in Russia, Australia, in Haiti, Soweto,
in Grenada, in Cuba, in Panama, Libya,
in England and Italy, France.

We are graces in any places.
I am Black and A Black
forever.

I am other than Hyphenation.

I say, proudly, MY PEOPLE!
I say, proudly, OUR PEOPLE!

Our People do not disdain to eat yams or melons or grits
or to put peanut butter in stew.

I am Kojo. In West Afrika Kojo
means Unconquerable. My parents
named me the seventh day from my birth
in Black spirit, Black faith, Black communion.
I am Kojo. I am A Black.
And I Capitalize my name.

Do not call me out of my name.

RELIGION

At home we pray every morning, we
get down on our knees in a circle,
holding hands, holding Love,
and we sing Hallelujah.

Then we go into the World.

Daddy **speeds**, to break bread with his Girl Friend.
Mommy's a Boss. And a lesbian.
(She too has a nice Girl Friend.)

My brothers and sisters and I come to school.
We bring knives pistols bottles, little boxes, and cans.

We talk to the man who's cool at the playground gate.
Nobody Sees us, nobody stops our sin.

Our teachers feed us geography.
We spit it out in a hurry.

Now we are coming home.

At home, we pray every evening, we
get down on our knees in a circle,
holding hands, holding Love.

And we sing Hallelujah.

UNCLE SEAGRAM

My uncle likes me too much.

I am five and a half years old, and in kindergarten.
In kindergarten everything is clean.

My uncle is six feet tall with seven bumps on his chin.
My uncle is six feet tall, and he stumbles.
He stumbles because of his Wonderful Medicine
packed in his pocket all times.

Family is ma and pa and my uncle,
three brothers, three sisters, and me.

Every night at my house we play checkers and dominoes.
My uncle sits <u>close</u>.
There aren't any shoes or socks on his feet.
Under the table a big toe tickles my ankle.
Under the oilcloth his thin knee beats into mine.
And mashes. And mashes.

When we look at TV
my uncle picks <u>me</u> to sit on his lap.
As I sit, he gets hard in the middle.
I squirm, but he keeps me, and kisses my ear.

I am not even a girl.

Once, when I went to the bathroom,
my uncle noticed, came in, shut the door,
put his long white tongue in my ear,
and whispered "We're Best Friends, and Family,
and we know how to keep Secrets."

My uncle likes me too much. I am worried.

I do not like my uncle anymore.

IN EAST AFRIKA SALA MEANS GENTLENESS

And I admire to be Gentle.

But I am sucked into earth.
(I have seen, in the movies, the quicksand.)
But I am whipped through the wind.
(I have seen, in the movies, the hurricane, hot-moving Gray.)
But I am drowning, oddly, in an odd ocean.
(I have seen, in the movies, Moby Dick.)

Well, now I am coming home.
I shall be better
after the aspirin and wine.

IN THE PERSIAN GULF

Teacher told us today of those people in the Persian Gulf.

The people
bent over babies.
The people
worked with wheelbarrow and word-processor;
went into mines.
The people made love.
twisting into comical curlicues.
They birthdayed, prayed,
said,
marketed,
watched rich men and robbers,
ate okra and rice, ate bread.

A wedding was colors and honor and music and magic.

In the afternoons
It was just dear: little bunches of people, laughing sometimes.
The people had chocolate,
had cocoa.
Their rich eyes lit, met.
They talked of their here, their hereafter.
They talked of their hometime killers, in symbols or softly.

Then the Other Killers came.

SONG: WHITE POWDER

They want me to take the white powder.
I won't, so they beat me.

They want me to deal the white powder.
I won't, so they beat me.

They tell me I'll hot-pile the Money.
They tell me my Power will roll.
They tell me I'll rule my own runners.
I'll be Mighty. I'll be
IN CONTROL.

When I say "Hot at eleven, cold before twelve"
they beat me.

ABRUPTLY

God is a gorilla.

I see him standing in the sky.
He is clouds.
There's a beard that is
white and light gray.

His arms are gorilla arms,
limp at his sides; his fists
not easy but not angry.

I tell my friend.
Pointing, I tell my friend
"God is a gorilla. Look!
There!"

My friend says "It is a crime
to call God a gorilla. You have insulted our God."

I answer:
"Gorilla is majesty.
Other gorillas
know."

QUESTIONS

Home is a Shape before me.
I travel three blocks to Home.

Are the dishes in the sink, still,
with morning yellow dried on?
And
is there <u>another</u> color in the kitchen?
(The kitchen is where he whips her.)
Is red all over Mama once again?
Is pa still Home, with a mean and sliding mouth?
With hands like hams.
With
stares that are scissors, tornadoes.

Fleur

OUR WHITE MOTHER SAYS WE ARE BLACK BUT NOT VERY

My brother and I are Nice People.
We are Black, but we have creamy skin.
We have hair that is naturally curly.
We wear jackets and shoes that cost lots of money.
Our lunch box was hammered in Holland.
We live in the biggest house on our street
and will move Very Soon to a Special Neighborhood
But even in this house we have shelves and shelves,
we have cases and cases of books with fine bindings,
And sometimes we even read them. Our father
speaks six languages, our mother speaks three.
Each of us takes at least two showers a day.

We simply cannot abide smelly children
or children with dull hurt eyes.

My brother and I will grow up to be
doctors or lawyers or Supreme Court Justices
or perfume distributors or Wall Street wizards.
Or the ones who discover the answer-to-cancer.

My brother and I do not have many friends, it is true.

But at Home we'll wait for High Tea.
Little scones with cinnamon butter,
salmon croquettes with flakes of green pepper,
little cucumber sandwiches, cashews,
sugar in cubes with our English Breakfast Tea.
Candied ginger.
And orange juice if we want it.

Diego

Puzzlement

"Black Pride" Day

I, partly Nigerian.
I, partly Puerto Rican.

I have a Nigerian father,
a Puerto Rican mother.
I am packed in a skin that is tan.

I, too, have a heart on fire.
I, too, want to be Proud.
I, too, want to be Something and Proud.

I want to shout "I'M A TAN!"

Martin D

BEST FRIENDS

Getting to home means joining
Very Best Friends____
from the very wide shelf
my father put on a wall for me.

One Friend, or another, knows what to say to me
on Monday, or Thursday,
for Monday or Thursday need.

If I want Repairing____
or something to lock me up____
or a happy key to open me____
or fire when school has made me crispy-cold____
Coming home
I choose

from Very Best Friends on the very wide shelf
my father put on a wall
for me.

MY BROTHERS GREET ME EVERY AFTERNOON

My brothers, Lay Low and Hip Slapper,
may do Better now.
Mo say they may.

They wailed much!
Behind those banging bars in the Jail
they wailed much.

Now they breathe fresh air
when they require.

Mo has to serve up beans and sweet potatoes,
wide waffles, peanut syrup
and a couple of dollars every day.

She say
"Men must have Money in they over-alls."

My brothers look me quickly at the eye,
quickly away.
They say
"Hey li'l bro. — you
watch yourself."

Two more pairs of twisty lips,
two more pairs of whipped-up eyes,
two more pairs of hands-in-pockets
decorate the corner now.

Tahanni

PET

I want to tell my puppy
what went All Wrong
today.

You can tell your puppy
a Too Much.

Aron

TO BE GROWN UP

The whole chocolate cake can be yours.

To be grown up means
you don't get a report card.
You don't face a father, a mother.

The walls of the cage are gone.
The fortress is done and down.

To be grown up means
the Bill will be paid by you.

To be grown up means
you can get sick and stay sick.
Your legs will not love you. They'll fail.

No icy sidewalks for sliding.

No grandmother to fix you big biscuits.
No grandfather to sing you "Asleep in the Deep."

A SOMETHING ALL MY OWN

I am already thinking
of my own death
as a Possession of MINE
after the Creation it <u>shall</u> surely be.

That will come my own.
That will happen Surely Mine.

I'LL STAY

I like the plates on the ledge
of the dining room wall (to the north)
standing on edge,
standing as if they thought they could stay.

Confident things can stand and stay!

I am confident.
I always thought there was something to be done about
everything.
I'll stay.
I'll not go pouting and shouting out of the city.
I'll stay.

My name will be Up In Lights!
I believe it!
They will know me as Nora-the-Wonderful!
It will happen!
I'll stay.

Mother says "You rise in the morning —
You must be the Sun!
For wherever <u>you</u> are there is Light,
and those who are near you are warm, feel Efficient."

I'll stay.

In The Mecca

**To the memory of Langston Hughes;
and to James Baldwin, Amiri Baraka.
and Mike Alexandroff,
educators extraordinaire.**

". . . a great gray hulk of brick, four stories high,
topped by an ungainly smokestack, ancient and enormous,
filling half the block north of Thirty-fourth Street
between State and Dearborn . . . the Mecca Building . . . .
The Mecca Building is U-shaped. The dirt courtyard is
littered with newspapers and tin cans, milk cartons and
broken glass. . . . Iron fire escapes run up the building's
face and ladders reach from them to the roof. There are
four main entrances, two on Dearborn and two on State
Street. At each is a gray stone threshold and over
each is carved "THE MECCA." (The Mecca was constructed
as an apartment building in 1891, a splendid palace,
a showplace of Chicago. . . .)"
—JOHN BARTLOW MARTIN

"How many people live here? . . . Two thousand? oh, more
than that. There's 176 apartment and some of 'em's got
seven rooms and they're all full."
—A MECCAN

". . . . there's danger in my neighborhood . . ."
—RICHARD "PEANUT" WASHINGTON

"There comes a time when what has been can never be again."
—RUSS MEEK

IN TRIBUTE—

Jim Cunningham, Jim Taylor, Mike Cook,
Walter Bradford, Don Lee, Curtis Ellis,
Roy Lewis, Peggy Susberry, Ronda Davis,
Carolyn Rodgers, Sharon Scott,
Alicia Johnson, Jewel Latimore

Now the way of the Mecca was on this wise.

Sit where the light corrupts your face.
Miës Van der Rohe retires from grace.
And the fair fables fall.

S. Smith is Mrs. Sallie, Mrs. Sallie
hies home to Mecca, hies to marvelous rest;
ascends the sick and influential stair.
The eye unrinsed, the mouth absurd
with the last sourings of the master's Feast.
She plans
to set severity apart,
to unclench the heavy folly of the fist.
Infirm booms
and suns that have not spoken die behind this
low-brown butterball. Our prudent partridge.
A fragmentary attar and armed coma.
A fugitive attar and a district hymn.

Sees old St. Julia Jones, who has had prayer,
and who is rising from amenable knees
inside the wide-flung door of 215.
"Isn't He wonderfulwonderful!" cries St. Julia.
"Isn't our Lord the greatest to the brim?
The light of my life. And I lie late
past the still pastures. And meadows. He's the comfort
and wine and piccalilli for my soul.
He hunts me up the coffee for my cup.
Oh how I love that Lord."

          And Mrs. Sallie,
all innocent of saints and signatures,
nods and consents, content to endorse
Lord as an incense and a vintage. Speaks
to Prophet Williams, young beyond St. Julia,
and rich with Bible, pimples, pout: who reeks
with lust for his disciple, is an engine
of candid steel hugging combustibles.
His wife she was a skeleton.
His wife she was a bone.
Ida died in self-defense.
(Kinswomen!
Kinswomen!)
Ida died alone.

Out of her dusty threshold bursts Hyena.
The striking debutante. A fancier of firsts.
One of the first, and to the tune of hate,
in all the Mecca to paint her hair sun-gold.
          And Mrs.
Sallie sees Alfred. Ah, his God!—
To create! To create! To bend with the tight intentness
over the neat detail, come to
a terrified standstill of the heart, then shiver,
then rush—successfully—
at that rebuking thing, that obstinate and
recalcitrant little beast, the phrase!

To have the joy of deciding—successfully—
how stuffs can be compounded or sifted out
and emphasized, what the importances are;
what coats in which to wrap things. Alfred is un-
talented. Knows, Marks time and themes at Phillips,
stares, glares, of mornings, at a smear
which does not care what he may claim or doubt
or probe or clear or want, or what he might have been.
He "fails" no one; at faculty lunch hour
allows the zoology teacher, who has great legs,
to fondle him and curse his pretty hair. He
reads Shakespeare in the evenings or reads Joyce
or James or Horace, Huxley, Hemingway.
Later, he goes to bed with Telly Bell
in 309, or with that golden girl,
or thinks, or drinks until the Everything
is vaguely a part of One thing and the One thing
delightfully anonymous
and undiscoverable. So he is weak,
is weak, is no good. Never mind.
It is a decent enough no-goodness. And it is
a talkative, curly, charitable, spiced weakness
which makes a woman in charge of zoology
dream furiously at night.
When there were all those gods
administering to panthers,
jumping over mountains,

and lighting stars and comets and a moon,
what was their one Belief?
what was their joining thing?

A boy breaks glass and Mrs. Sallie
rises to the final and fourth floor.

Children, what she has brought you is hock of ham.
She puts the pieces to boil in white enamel, right
already with water of many seasonings, at the back
of the cruel stove. And mustard mesmerized by
eldest daughter, the Undaunted (she who once
pushed her thumbs in the eyes of a Thief), awaits
the clever hand. Six ruddy yams abide, and
cornbread made with water.

Now Mrs. Sallie
confers her bird-hat to her kitchen table,
and sees her kitchen. It is bad, is bad,
her eyes say, and My soft antagonist,
her eyes say, and My headlong tax and mote,
her eyes say, and My maniac default,
my least light.
"But all my lights are little!"
Her denunciation
slaps savagely not only this sick kitchen but
her Lord's annulment of the main event.

"I want to decorate!" But what is that? A
pomade atop a sewage. An offense.
First comes correctness, *then* embellishment!
And music, mode, and mixed philosophy
may follow fitly on propriety
to tame the whiskey of our discontent!
"What can I do?"
   But World (a sheep)
wants to be Told.
If you ask a question, you
can't stop there.
You must keep going.
You can't stop there: World will
waive; will be
facetious, angry. You can't stop there.
You have to keep on going.

Doublemint as a protective device. Yvonne
prepares for her lover.
Gum is something he can certify.
Gum is something he can understand.
A tough girl gets it. A rough
Ruthie or Sue. It is unembarrassable,
and will seem likely. It is very bad,
but in its badness it is nearly grand,
and is a crown that tops bald innocence
and gentle fright.

It is not necessary, says Yvonne,
to have every day him whom
to the end thereof you will love.
Because it is tasty to remember
he is alive, and laughs
in somebody else's room,
or is slicing a cold cucumber,
or is buttoning his cuffs,
or is signing with his pen
and will plan
to touch you again.

Melodie Mary hates everything pretty and plump.
And Melodie, Cap and Casey
and Thomas Earl, Tennessee, Emmett and Briggs
hate sewn suburbs;
hate everything combed and strong; hate people who
have balls, dolls, mittens and dimity frocks and trains
and boxing gloves, picture books, bonnets for Easter.
Lace handkerchief owners are enemies of Smithkind.

Melodie Mary likes roaches,
and pities the gray rat.
To delicate Melodie Mary
headlines are secondary.
It is interesting that in China
the children blanch and scream,

and that blood runs like a ragged wound
through the ancient flesh of the land.
It matters, mildly,
that the Chinese girls are grim,
and that hurried are the seizures
of yellow hand on hand. . . .
What if they drop like the tumbling tears
of the old and intelligent sky?
Where are the frantic bulletins
when other importances die?
Trapped in his privacy of pain
the worried rat expires.
and smashed in the grind of a rapid heel
last night's roaches lie.

Briggs is adult as a stone
(who if he cries cries alone).
The Gangs are out, but he must go
to and fro,
appease what reticences move
across the intemperate range.
Immunity is forfeit, love
is luggage, hope is heresy.
Gang
is health and mange.
Gang
is a bunch of ones and a singlicity.
Please pity Briggs. But there is a central height in pity
past which man's hand and sympathy cannot go;

past which the little hurt dog
descends to mass—no longer Joe,
not Bucky, not Cap'n, not Rex,
not Briggs—and is all self-employed,
concerned with Other,
not with Us.
Briggs, how "easy," finally, to accept (after the shriek and repulsion)
the unacceptable evil. To proceed with some eclat;
some salvation of the face;
awake! to choke the chickens, file their blood.

One reason cats are happier than people
is that they have no newspapers. . . I must be,
culls Tennessee,
like my cat, content to gaze
at men and women spurting here and there.
I must sit, let
them stroke me as and when they will;
must drink their milk and cry
for meat. At other times I must be still.
Who tingles in
and mixes with affairs and others met
comes out with scratches and is very thin
and rides the red possession of regret.

        In the midst
of hells and gruels and little halloweens

tense Thomas Earl loves Johnny Appleseed.
"I, Johnny Appleseed."
It is hard to be Johnny Appleseed.
The ground shudders.
The ground springs up;
hits you with gnarls and rust,
derangement and fever, or blare and clerical treasons.

Emmett and Cap and Casey
are skin wiped over bones
for lack of chub and chocolate
and ice cream cones,
for lack of English muffins
and boysenberry jam.
What shall their redeemer be?
Greens and hock of ham.
For each his greens and hock of ham
and a spoon of sweet potato.

Alfred says:
The faithless world!
betraying yet again
trinities!
My chaste displeasure
is not enough;
the brilliant British of the new command
is not enough;

the counsels of division, the hot counsels,
the scuffle and short pout
are not enough, are only
a pressure of clankings and affinities
against
the durable fictions of a Charming Trash.
Mrs. Sallie
evokes and loves and loathes a pink-lit image
of the toy-child. Her Lady's.
Her Lady's pink convulsion, toy-child dances
in stiff wide pink through Mrs. Sallie. Stiff pink is
on toy-child's poverty of cream
under a shiny tended warp of gold.
What shiny tended gold is an aubade
for toy-child's head! Has ribbons too!
Ribbons. Not Woolworth cotton comedy,
not rubber band, not string. . . .
"And that would be my baby be my baby. . . .
And I would be my lady I my lady . . . ."

What else is there to say but everything?

SUDDENLY, COUNTING NOSES, MRS. SALLIE
SEES NO PEPITA. "WHERE PEPITA BE?"

. . . Cap, where Pepita? Casey, where Pepita?
Emmett and Melodie Mary, where Pepita?

Briggs, Tennessee, Yvonne, and Thomas Earl,
where may our Pepita be?—
our Woman with her terrible eye,
with iron and feathers in her feet,
with all her songs so lemon-sweet,
with lightning and a candle too
and junk and jewels too?
My heart begins to race.
I fear the end of Peace.

Ain seen er I ain seen er I ain seen er
Ain seen er I ain seen er I ain seen er

Yvonne up-ends her iron. And is constrained.
Cannot now conjure love-within-the-park.
Cannot now conjure spice and soft explosion
mixing with miffed mosquitoes where the dark
defines and re-defines.

    And Melodie Mary
and Thomas Earl and Tennessee and Briggs
yield cat-contentment gangs rats Appleseed.

Emmett and Cap and Casey
yield visions of vice and veal,
dimes and windy carnival,
candied orange peel,

peppermint in a pickle;
and where the ladybug
glistens in her leaf-hammock; *light*
lasses to hiss and hug.

And they are constrained. All are constrained.
    And there is no thinking of grapes or gold
    or of any wicked sweetness and they ride
    upon fright and remorse and their stomachs
    are rags or grit.
In twos!
In threes! Knock-knocking down the martyred halls
at doors behind whose yelling oak or pine
    many flowers start, choke, reach up,
    want help, get it, do not get it,
    rally, bloom, or die on the wasting vine.

"One of my children is missing. One of my children is gone."

Great-great Gram hobbles, fumbles at the knob,
mumbles, "I ain seen no Pepita. But
I remember our cabin. The floor was dirt.
And something crawled in it. That is the thought
stays in my mind. I do not recollect
what 'twas. But something. Something creebled in that dirt
for we wee ones to pop. Kept popping at it.
Something that squishied. *Then* your heel come down!

I hear them squishies now. . . . *Pop*, Pernie May!
That's sister Pernie. That's my sister Pernie.
Squish. . . . Out would jump her little heel.
And that was the end of Something. Sister Pernie
was our best popper. Pern and me and all,
we had no beds. Some slaves had beds of hay
or straw, with cover-cloth. We six-uns curled
in corners of the dirt, and closed our eyes,
and went to sleep—or listened to the rain
fall inside, felt the drops
big on our noses, bummies and tum-tums. . . ."

Although he has not seen Pepita, Loam
Norton considers Belsen and Dachau,
regrets all old unkindnesses and harms.
. . . The Lord was their shepherd.
Yet did they want.
Joyfully would they have lain in jungles or pastures,
walked beside waters. Their gaunt
souls were not restored, their souls were banished.
In the shadow valley
they feared the evil, whether with or without God.
They were comforted by no Rod,
no Staff, but flayed by, O besieged by, shot a-plenty.
The prepared table was the rot or curd of the day.
Anointings were of lice. Blood was the spillage of cups.
Goodness and mercy should follow them
        all the days of their death.

They should dwell in the house of the Lord forever
and, dwelling, save a place for me.
I am not remote,
not unconcerned. . . .

Boontsie De Broe has
not seen Pepita Smith: but is
a Lady
among Last Ladies.
Erect. Direct.
An engraving on the crowd, the blurred crowd.
She is away and fond.
Her clear voice tells you life may be controlled.
Her clear mind is the extract
of massive literatures, of lores,
transactions of old ocean; suffrages.

Yvonne
recovers to aver
despite the stomp of the stupor.
        She will not go
in Hudson's hashhouse. And the Tivoli
is a muffler of Love.
In the blasé park,
that winks and mocks but is at all times
tolerant of the virtuous defect, of audit,
        and of mangle and of wile, he

may permit perusal of their ground,
its rubble-over-rose: may look to rainbow:
may sanction bridal tulle, white flowers,
may allow a mention of a minister and twins. . . .

        But *other* Smiths are twitching. They recall
vain vagrants, recall old peddlers, young fine bumlets,
The Man Who Sells The Peaches Plums Bananas.
They recall the Fuller Brush Man,
oblique and delicate, who tries on
the very fit and feature of despair.
"Pepita's smart," says Sallie; her stretched eyes
reject the exact despatches of a mind turned boiler,
epithet, foiler, guillotine. *What*
of the Bad Old Man? The lover-like young man? The
half-mad boy who put his hand across Pepita's knee?
"Pepita's smart," says Sallie.
Knowing the ham hocks are burning at the bottom of the pan.

S. and eight of her children reach their door. The
door says, "What are you doing here? And where
is Pepita the puny—the halted, glad-sad-child?"
They pet themselves, subdue
the legislation of their yoke and devils.
        Has just wandered!
        Has just blundered

away
from her own.
And there's no worry
that's necessary.
She
comes soon alone.
Comes soon alone or will be brought by neighbor.
Kind neighbor.

"Kind neighbor." They consider.
Suddenly
every one in the world is Mean.
Could that old woman, passively passing, mash a child?
Has she a tot's head in that shiny bag?
And that lank fellow looking furtive.
What
cold poison could he spew, what stench commit
upon a little girl, a little lost girl,
lone and languid in the world, wanting
her ma, her glad-sad, her Yvonne?

Emmett runs down the hall.
Emmett seizes John Tom's telephone.
(Despite the terror and the derivation,
despite the not avuncular frontier,
John Tom, twice forty in 420, claims
Life sits or blazes in this Mecca.

And thereby—tenable.
And thereby beautiful.)

Provoking calm and dalliance of the Law.
How shall the Law allow for littleness!
How shall the Law enchief the chapters of
wee brown-black chime, wee brown-black chastity?

The Law arrives—and does not quickly go
to fetch a Female of the Negro Race.
A lariat of questions.
The Mother screams and wants her baby. Wants her baby,
and wants her baby wants her baby.

Law leaves, with likeness of a "southern" belle. Sheriffs,
South State Street is a Postulate!
Until you look. You look—and you discover
the paper dolls are terrible. You touch.
You look and touch.
The paper dolls are terrible and cold.

Aunt Dill arrives to help them. "Little gal got
raped and choked to death last week. Her gingham
was tied around her neck and it was red
but had been green before with pearls and dots
of rhinestone on the collar, and her tongue
was hanging out (a little to the side);

her eye was all a-pop, one was; was one
all gone. Part of her little nose was gone
(bit off, the Officer said). The Officer said
that something not quite right been done that girl.
Lived Langley: 'round the corner from my house."
Aunt Dill extends
sinister pianissimos and apples,
and at that moment of the Thousand Souls is
a Christ-like creature, Doing Good.

The Law returns. It trots about the Mecca.
It pounds a dozen doors.

No, Alfred has not seen Pepita Smith.
But he (who might have been an architect)
can speak of Mecca: firm arms surround
disorders, bruising ruses and small hells,
small semiheavens: hug barbarous rhetoric
built of buzz, coma and petite pell-mells.
No, Alfred has not seen Pepita Smith.
But he (who might have been a poet-king)
can speak superbly of the line of Leopold.
The line of Leopold is thick with blackness
        and Scriptural drops and rises.
The line of Leopold is busy with betrothals of royal rage
        and conditional pardon and with
refusal of mothballs for outmoded love.

126

Senghor will not shred
love,
gargantuan gardens careful in the sun,
fairy story gold, thrones, feasts, the three princesses,
summer sailboats
like cartoon ghosts of Klansmen, pointing up
white questions, in blue air. . . .
No.
Believes in beauty.
But believes that blackness is among the fit filters.
Old cobra
coughs and curdles in his lungs,
spits spite, spits exquisite spite, and cries, "Ignoble!"
Needs "negritude."
Senghor (in Europe rootless and lonely) sings in art-lines
of Black woman.
Senghor sighs and, "negritude" needing,
speaks for others, for brothers. Alfred can tell of
Poet, and muller, and President of Senegal, who
in voice and body
loves sun,
listens
to the rich pound in and beneath the black feet of Africa.

Hyena, the striking debutante, is back;
bathed, used by special oils and fumes, will be
off to the Ball tonight. She has not seen
Pepita—"a puny and a putrid little child."

Death is easy.
It may come quickly,
It may come when nobody is ready.
Death may come at any time. Mazola
has never known Pepita S. But knows
the strangest thing is when the stretcher goes!—
the elegant hucksters bearing the body when the body
leaves its late lair the last time leaves.
With no plans for return.

Don Lee wants
not a various America.
Don lee wants
a new nation
under nothing;
a physical light that waxes; he does not want to
be exorcised, adjoining and revered;
he does not like a local garniture
nor any impish onus in the vogue;
is not candlelit
but strands out in the auspices of fire
and rock and jungle-flail;
wants
new art and anthem; will
want a new music screaming in the sun.

Says Alfred:
To be a red bush!
In the West Virginia autumn.
To flame out red.
"Crimson: is not word enough,
although close to what I mean.
How proud.
How proud.
(But the bush does not know it flames.)

"Takes time," grated the gradualist.
"Starting from when?" asked Amos.
Amos (not Alfred) says,
"Shall we sit on ourselves; shall we wait behind roses and veils
for monsters to maul us,
        for bulls to come butt us forever and ever,
shall we scratch in our blood,
        point air-powered hands at our wounds,
reflect on the aim of our bulls?" And Amos
(not Alfred) prays, for America prays:
"Bathe her in her beautiful blood.
A long blood bath will wash her pure.
Her skin needs special care.
Let this good rage continue out beyond
her power to believe or to surmise.
Slap the false sweetness from that face.

Great-nailed boots
must kick her prostrate, heel-grind that soft breast,
outrage her saucy pride,
remove her fair fine mask.
Let her lie there, panting and wild, her pain
red, running roughly through the illustrious ruin—
with nothing to do but think, think
of how she was so long grand,
flogging her dark one with her own hand,
watching in meek amusement while he bled.
Then shall she rise, recover.
Never to forget."

The ballad of Edie Barrow:
      I fell in love with a Gentile boy.
All creamy-and-golden fair.
He looked deep and long in my long black eyes.
And he played with my long black hair.
He took me away to his summertime house.
He was wondrous wealthy, was he.
And there in the hot black drapes of night
he whispered, "Good lovers are we."
Close was our flesh through the winking hours,
closely and sweetly entwined.
Love did not guess in the tight-packed dark
it was flesh of varying kind.
Scarletly back when the hateful sun

came bragging across the town.
And I could have killed the gentle Gentile
who waited to strap him down.
He will wed her come fall, come falling of fall.
And she will be queen of his rest.
I shall be queen of his summerhouse storm.
A hungry tooth in my breast.

"Pepita who?" And Prophet Williams yawns.
Prophet Williams' office in the Mecca
has a soiled window and a torn front sign.
His suit is shabby and slick.
He is not poor (clothes do *not* make the man).
He has a lawyer named Enrico Jason,
who talks. The Prophet advertises
in every Colored journal in the world. . . .
An old woman wants
from the most reverend Prophet of all prophets
a piece of cloth, licked by his Second Tongue,
to wrap around her paralytic leg.
Men with malicious sweethearts, evil sweethearts—
bringers of bad, bringers of tedium—
want Holy Thunderbolts, and Love Balls too.
And all want lucky numbers all the time.
Mallie (the Superintendent of six secretaries)
types. Mallie alone may know
the Combinations:

14-15-16
and 13-14-15. . . .
(magic is cut-out Number Forty-three).
Prophet will help you hold your Job, solve problems,
and, like a Sister Stella in Blue Island,
"can call your friends and enemies by name
without a single clue."
There is no need to visit in Blue Island.
Prophet will give you trading stamps and kisses,
or a cigar.
One visit will convince you.
Lucky days
and Lucky Hands. Lifts you
from Sorrow and the Shadows. Heals the body.
A sister Marlo on east Sixty-third
announces One
Visit Can Keep You Out of the Insane Asylum,
but
she stocks no Special Holiday Blessings for
Columbus Day and Christmas, nor keeps off
green devils and orange witches with striped fangs.
Prophet
has Drawing and Holding Powder, Attraction Powder, Black
Cat Powder, powerful Serum,
"Marvelous Potency Number Ninety-one"
(which stoppeth husbands and lovers from dastardy),
Pay-check Fluid, Running-around Elixir,

Policy Number Compeller, Voodoo Potion.
Enrico Jason, a glossy circular blackness, who
sees Lawmen and enhances Lawmen, soon
will like beside his Prophet in bright blood,
a rhythm of stillness
above the nuances.

How may care, Pepita?—
Staley and Lara,
the victim grasped, the harlot had and gone?
Eunie, the intimate tornado?
Simpson, the peasant king, Bixby and June,
the hollowed, the scant, the
played-out deformities? The margins?
Not those.
Not these three Maries
with warm unwary mouths and asking eyes
wide open, full of vagueness and surprise;
the limp ladies
(two in awful combat now:
a terrible battle of the Old:
speechless and physical: oh horrible
the obscene gruntings
the dull outwittings
the flabby semi-rhythmic shufflings
the blear starings
the small spittings).

Not Great-uncle Beer, white-headed twinkly man!—
laugher joker gambler killer too.
Great-uncle Beer says, "Casey Jones.
Yes, Casey Jones is still alive,
a chicken on his head."
Not Wezlyn, the wandering woman, the woman who wanders
the halls of the Mecca at night, in search
of Lawrence and Love.
                    Not Insane Sophie! If
you scream, you're marked "insane."
But silence is a *place* in which to scream!
Hush.
An agitation in the bush.
Occluded trees.
Mad life heralding the blue heat of God
snickers in a corner of the west windowsill.
"What have I done, and to the world,
        and to the love I promised Mother?"
An agitation in occluded trees.
The fires run up. Things slant.
The pillow's wet.
The fires run down and flatten.
(The grilles will dance over glass!)
You're marked "insane."
You cower.
Suddenly you're no longer
well-dressed. You're not

pretty in halls.
Like the others you want love, but
a cage in imminent.
Your doll is near. And will go with you.
Your doll, whom none will stun.

. . . How many care, Pepita?
Does Darkara?
Darkara looks at *Vogue.* Darkara sees
a mischievous impromptu and a sheen.
(In Palm Beach, Florida, Laddie Sanford say:
"I call it My Ocean. Of Course, it's the Atlantic.")
The painter, butcher, stockyards man, the Typist,
Aunt Tippie, Zombie Bell,
Mr. Kelly with long gray hair who begs
subtly from door to door, Gas Cady
the man who robbed J. Harrison's grave of mums
and left the peony bush only because
it was too big (said Mama), the janitor
who is a Political Person, Queenie King who
is an old poem silvering the noise,
and Wallace Williams who knows the
Way the Thing Is Supposed To Be Done—
these little care, Pepita, what befalls a
nullified saint or forfeiture (or child).

Alfred's Impression — his Apologie—
his Invocation—and his Ecstasie:
"Not Baudelaire, Bob Browning, not Neruda.
Giants over Steeples
are wanted in this Crazy-eyes, this Scar.
A violent reverse.
We part from all we thought we knew of love
and of dismay-with-flags-on. What we know
is that there are confusion and conclusion.
Rending.
Even the hardest parting is a contribution. . . .
What shall we say?
Farewell, And Hail! Until Farewell again."

Officers!—
do you nearly wish you had not come into this room?
The sixtyish sisters, the twins with the floured faces,
who dress in long stiff blackness,
who exit stiffly together and enter together
stiffly,
muffle their Mahler, finish their tea,
stare at the lips of the Law—
but have not seen Pepita anywhere.
They pull on their long white gloves,
they flour their floured faces,
and stiffly leave Law and the Mecca.

Way-out Morgan is collecting guns
in a tiny fourth-floor room.
He is not hungry, ever, though sinfully lean.
He flourishes, ever, on porridge or pat of bean
pudding or wiener soup—fills fearsomely
on visions of Death-to-the-Hordes-of-the-White-Men!
Death!
(This is the Maxim painted in big black
above a bed bought at a Champlain rummage sale.)
Remembering three local-and-legal beatings, he
rubs his hands in glee,
does Way-out Morgan, Remembering his Sister
mob-raped in Mississippi, Way-out Morgan
smacks sweet his lips and adds another gun
and listens to Blackness stern and blunt and beautiful,
organ-rich Blackness telling a terrible story.
Way-out Morgan
predicts the Day of Debt-pay shall begin,
the Day of Demon-diamond,
of blood in mouths and body-mouths,
of flesh-rip in the Forum of Justice at last!
Remembering mates in the Mississippi River,
mates with black bodies once majestic, Way-out
postpones a yellow woman in his bed, postpones
wetnesses and little cries and stomachings—
to consider Ruin.

"Pepita? No."
Marian is mixing.
Take Marian mixing. Gumbo File or roux.
At iron: at ire with faucet, husband, young.
Knows no
gold hour.
Sings
but sparsely, and subscribes to axioms
atop her gargoyles and tamed foam. Good axioms.
Craves crime: her murder, her deep wounding, or
a leprosy so lovely as to pop
the slights and sleep of her community,
her Mecca.
A Thing. To make the people heel and stop
and See her.
Never strides
about, up!
Never alters earth or air!
Her children cannot quake, be proud.
Her husband never Saw her, never said
her single silver certain Self aloud.

Pops Pinkham, forgetting Pepita,
is somewhat doubtful of a specific right
to inherit the earth or to partake of it now. . . .

Old women should not seek to be perfumed, said Plutarch.

But Dill, the kind of woman you
peek at in passing and thank your God or zodiac you
may never have to know, puts on *Tabu*.
Aunt Dill is happy. Nine years Little Papa
has been completely at rest in Lincoln Cemetery.
Children were stillbirths all. Aunt Dill
has bits of brass and marble, and Franciscan
china; has crocheted doilies; has old mahogany,
polished till it burns with a smothered glow; has
antimacassars, spreads, silk draperies,
her silver creamer and her iron lamp,
her piece of porcelain, her seventeen
Really Nice handkerchiefs pressed in cedar. Dill
is woman-in-love-with-God.
Is not
true-child-of-God——for are we ever to
be children?——are we never to mature,
be lovely lovely? be soft Woman
rounded and darling . . . almost caressable . . .
and certainly wearing *Tabu* in the name of the Lord.
Dill straightens—tries to forget the hand of God
(. . . which would be skillful . . . would be flattering . . .)

    I hate it.
    Yet, murmurs Alfred—
who is lean at the balcony, leaning—
something, something in Mecca

continues to call! Substanceless; yet like mountains,
like rivers and oceans too; and like trees
with wind whistling through them. And steadily
an essential sanity, black and electric,
builds to a reportage and redemption.
  A hot estrangement.
  A material collapse
that is Construction.

Hateful things sometimes befall the hateful
but the hateful are not rendered lovable thereby.
The murderer of Pepita
looks at the Law unlovably. Jamaican
Edward denies and thrice denies a dealing
of any dimension with Mrs. Sallie's daughter.
  Beneath his cot
a little woman lies in dust with roaches.
She never went to kindergarten.
She never learned that black is not beloved.
Was royalty when poised,
sly, at the A and P's fly-open door.
Will be royalty no more.
"I touch"—she said once—"petals of a rose.
A silky feeling through me goes!"
Her mother will try for roses.

She whose little stomach fought the world had
wriggled, like a robin!
Odd were the little wrigglings
and the chopped chirpings oddly rising.

140

Gwendolyn Elizabeth Brooks

GWENDOLYN ELIZABETH BROOKS
1917 - 2000

Gwendolyn Brooks was born in Topeka, Kansas on June 7, 1917. Her family returned to Chicago, Illinois, shortly after her birth, and her parents nurtured her love of literature at an early age. Ms. Brooks graduated from Englewood High School and received an Associates Degree from Wilson Junior College, now known as Kennedy-King College, in 1936. She met Henry Blakely, a fellow writer and businessman at an NAACP poetry group. They were married in 1939 and had two children, Henry Jr. and Nora.

Ms. Brooks conducted seminars, workshops and readings at countless major educational institutions across the country and taught at several including the University of Wisconsin-Madison, City College of New York, Columbia College of Chicago, Northeastern Illinois University, and Elmhurst College. At the time of her death, Ms. Brooks had been the Distinguished Professor of English at Chicago State University for several years and the Poet Laureate of Illinois since 1969.

Ms. Brooks' lifelong career enhanced, enriched, and embraced language on an international scale. She was awarded over 75 honorary doctorates and was a much-sought after speaker known for her giving, compassionate, (and sometimes mischievous) spirit.

Ms. Brooks authored more than twenty books of poetry including *A Street in Bronzeville* (1945), *Selected Poems* (1963), *In the Mecca* (1968), *Riot* (1969), *The Tiger Who Wore White Gloves* (1970), *Blacks* (1987), and *Children Coming Home* (1992). She also wrote one novel, *Maud Martha* (1953), two autobiographies, *Report from Part One: An Autobiography* (1972) and *Report from Part Two: Autobiography* (1996), and edited *Jump Bad: A New Chicago Anthology* (1971).

In 1997, Mayor Richard M. Daley announced Gwendolyn Brooks Week in conjunction with her 80th birthday. A special program entitled Eighty Gifts was held at the Harold Washington Library Center with presentations by 80 writers and performers from across the globe. Other special honors include the Gwendolyn Brooks Center for Black Literature and Creative Writing at Chicago State University; the Gwendolyn Brooks Junior High School in Harvey, Illinois as well as schools named after her in Aurora and DeKalb, Illinois; the Gwendolyn Brooks Cultural Center at Western Illinois University in Macomb, Illinois; the Edward Jenner School Auditorium in Chicago's Cabrini-Green community, and the engraved listing of her name on the Carter G. Woodson Regional Library in Chicago and the Illinois State Library in Springfield.

Ms. Brooks' had a special commitment to young people and sponsored various poetry awards, including the Illinois Poet Laureate Awards, an annual event she developed and ran for over 30 years to honor young writers from Illinois elementary schools and high schools. This project, along with many other programs, contests, and events were personally financed by Ms. Brooks in her efforts to give writers opportunities to publicly read their writings, receive monetary awards in recognition of their achievements, and be celebrated for their creative talent.

The legacy of Gwendolyn Brooks consists of her immeasurable contributions to literature as well as the cultural and social contributions made by those she influenced in myriad ways.

Selected awards and honors

Pulitzer Prize for Literature (1950)
Poet Laureate of Illinois (1969-2000)
29th Consultant in Poetry to the Library of Congress
(1985-1986)
Senior Fellowship in Literature (1989) by the National
Endowment for the Arts
Medal for Distinguished Contributions to American Letters by
the National Book Foundation (1994)
Jefferson Lecturer from the National Endowment for the
Humanities Lifetime Achievement Award (1994)
National Medal of Art (1995)
Lincoln Laureate Award (1997)
International Literary Hall of Fame for Writers of African
Descent (1998)
65th Academy Fellowship from The Academy of American Poets
(2000)

A U R O R A

"the early period of anything"
Webster

by Gwendolyn Brooks

We who are weak and wonderful, wicked, bewildered, wistful and wild
are saying direct Good mornings through the fever.

It is the giant-hour.
Nothing less than gianthood will do:
nothing less than mover, prover, shover, cover, lever, diver,
for giant tacklings, overturnings, new
organic staring
that will involve, that will involve us all.

We say direct Good-mornings through the fever.
across the brooding obliques, the somersaults, ashes,
across
the importances stylishly killed:
across
the edited bias.
the waffling of woman.
the structured rejection of blackness.

Ready for ways.
windows:
remodeling spirals; closing the hot cliches.
Unwinding witchcraft.

Opening to sun.

Broadside No. 65. Broadside Series
Copyright © 1972 by Gwendolyn Brooks Blakely
All Rights Reserved
Broadside Press, Detroit, Michigan